WHISPERS OF MY SOUL

WHISPERS OF MY SOUL

Cecile Yael Lubin Dumornay

iUniverse, Inc.
New York   Bloomington

WHISPERS OF MY SOUL

iUniverse books may be ordered through booksellers or by contacting:

iUniverse
1663 Liberty Drive
Bloomington, IN 47403
www.iuniverse.com
1-800-Authors (1-800-288-4677)

ISBN: 978-1-4401-2555-3 (pbk)
ISBN: 978-1-4401-2556-0 (ebk)

Printed in the United States of America

iUniverse rev. date: 3/11/2009

BIOGRAPHY

I was born and raised in a tiny village on the south coast of Haiti, called Roche-a-Bateau (French for rock as a boat), so named due to a large rock, shaped as a boat, and adorned with plush green vegetation in the middle of the ocean, a few miles before the location of my actual birth town. I was immensely blessed to live my youngest years really close to nature: the ocean, mountains, rivers, sunrises and sunsets, moonrises and moonsets, native animals, trees, flowers, medicinal plants and others, and courageous, faith-filled, joyous folks. Hence, poetry has been the music of my soul as I dance through the peaks and valleys of my life. Though unexpressed for almost fifty years, it is now flowing out abundantly for me to enjoy and share here with the world. And for this precious gift, I am deeply grateful. I write on a variety of topics and themes, about whomever or whatever tickles my soul.

I completed my elementary and secondary education in my native Haiti, earned a teacher's certification, experienced five years as a nun in the convent of the Canadian Order of the Missionaries of the Immaculate Conception. Two years before I entered the convent, while I was there, and a year after I left, I taught elementary education for a total of seven years. In October 1983, I moved to the United States, joining my second older brother, living then in Dorchester, MA. As a new immigrant in this country, for the first year, I learned English mainly with PBS "Sesame Street" TV program, and through books, writing letters to imaginary friends in English, noting new words in my constant notebook companion while on the bus, at work, at the Post Office, or department stores, and taking English classes. That first year, I worked as housekeeper aid in various nursing homes in Massachusetts, then assisting the elderly in their homes, as a home health aid.

As I became more proficient in the English language, I worked three years as an administrative assistant in a Catholic school in Dorchester, MA, ten years as an ESOL teacher/counselor/ community liaison at The Community Learning Center in Cambridge, MA. While working in the latter position, I felt a deep yearning for something more, a different career. So, I decided to resume academic study, earned a Master's Degree in Marriage and Family Therapy from Cambridge College, Cambridge, MA, and obtained my national license as a Marriage & Family Therapist in Massachusetts two years later. Growing weary of the cold climate in that northern state, having divorced from my short-lived marriage to my then Jewish American husband, I relocated in tropical South Florida. There, I earned a Certificate for Addiction Professionals (CAP), fulfilled the requirements of the Professional Licensing Board of Florida, and re-obtainede my license as a Marriage & Family Therapist--since the State of Florida does not honor some licenses earned in other states. After a few more local changes in residence, I presently live in the beautiful city of Hollywood, FL, and have been working in the Substance Addiction Treatment field for over seven years. Here, I continue to enjoy nature, particularly the ocean, as much as, or perhaps more than I did growing up in my native Haiti.

FOREWORD & ACKNOWLEDGEMENTS

February 1, 2009, birthday of the late Langston Hughes, one of our most eminent African-American artist. Little did I realize the awe-filled synchronicity when I set aside this day to submit my manuscript to iUniverse. Indeed, sending my poetry on this day to be published bears greater significance than what I originally thought. I was just thinking it's time and I want to do this on a weekend day for more free time to focus on this tremendous, exciting endeavor of my life. Then, as I switched my Black American History calendar to the month of February, lo' and behold, today is Mr. Langston Hughes' birthday! Thus, with great pride, honor, gratitude, and joy, I am saluting Mr. Langston Hughes with my first poetry book to be published, while still rejoicing over the monumental historical event of January 20, 2009, as the United States of America inaugurated our first African-American President, Barack Hussein Obama.

As I think of it, 2009 dawns as a year of great beginnings and exciting changes, propelling the world community to grow, perhaps kicking and screaming, in deeply positive ways. And here I come joining in this renewal movement, humble and elated, to share the Whispers of My Soul with all, hoping that each poem brings a smile, a blessing, an insight, or ignites hope in every person who reads it.

I want to thank God, the universe, my parents, my nine beautifully gifted siblings, my twenty-four nephews and nieces--some of them the subject of several of my poems-- my in-laws, my friends, my work colleagues, the rabbis, their families, and members of Jewish Renewal Temple Adath Or for their loving support; Broward County Public Library, my fellow members of the Writer's Group at the South Regional Library for their sensible feedback on several of my poems, this group's patient leader Peter K. Jarrett who volunteered his time and assistance; everyone and everything who/which provided me with inspiration, love and appreciation.

My gratitude also goes to the members of the Haitian Catholic choir, Alabanza, for their song celebrating life "Se Lavi", to which I enjoy my morning gratitude dance, and to iUniverse for allowing me to offer the Whispers of My Soul to share with the world through their publishing expertise.

SPECIAL DEDICATION

This book is lovingly dedicated to Mommy Adou (my mother, Marie Antoinette Adrienne Lubin Dumornay), Bout Chen (my father, Jean Emmanuel Chenier Dumornay) for giving me life and nurturing me so well that I am able to share my gift of poetry with others today. Best of health, wholeness, peace, and joy to both of you! Mwen renmen nou anpil! (I love you very much!)

MIRACLE SEEDS

Miracle seeds

Of all sizes

Colors, forms, and tones

The likes

Of the miraculous oil remnant

Celebrated through Jewish Chanukah

Miracle seed you are

Hanukkah baby

And I am

Miracle seeds

Within and around us

We hold

Should we bother

To look with inner eyes

Discover, appreciate

And be responsible

For the seeds

Within and around

Expose them

To the light of Love

For direction of growth

For nurturance and manifestation

Miracle seeds

Screaming to blossom

To be components

Joining in

The ultimate picture show

The glorious symphony

Of a full-blown glorious Universe!

A DATE WITH A BIRTH

Shhhhh!
In the still of the night
Like approaching a bird's nest
At the dawn of morning
Witness and player at once
Tiptoeing
In the still of the night
Watching my soul enfold
Peeling out of its strangely
Comfortable cocoon
Slowly honing and owning
Every breath of newness
Shedding off
 Bristles of old
Gently crackling off
Melting away into nothingness
In the still of the night

Shhhh!
A new me is dawning
And I am watching
My soul wide open
Waiting to exhale
To the whole wide world
Fresh and refreshing breath waves
Of
Transfigured Cecile

BREATHING BEING

Breathing into my toes
Breathing into my head
In every part in between
Breathing Being
Breathing wholeness
Into every nook and cranny
Where pain is hidden
Breathing Being
Breathing wholeness
Into my old wounds
My unresolved issues
Breathing Being
Breathing wholeness
Into my re-surging war declarations
Into my resisted emotions and fears
Shooting out
As pain in my bodies or phobias
Taking turns
Shrinking, paralyzing, freezing
My birth-given flow
Breathing Being
Breathing wholeness
Into my pain
In all shapes or forms
My anger, my feeling blues
My resentments, my fears
Frustration and hopelessness
Lack of faith and hesitations
Contradictions and self-loathing
My guilt, my self-pity
Lack of trust, trusting too much
My insecurities, anxieties
Feeling unworthy of this
Incapable of that

3

Sneaking in my daily functioning
Interfering with my being

Breathing Being
Breathing wholeness
Into my pain
Exorcizing all these demons
Pageants from the court
Of the booby prize king
Breathing Being
Breathing wholeness
As I dance my way
Through my journey
In resurrecting the real me
Breathing Being
Breathing wholeness
Exhaling toxic fumes
From poisoning death-marked experiences
Breathing Being
With exhilarating surges
Of sheer, impetuous Joy
Love, Peace, Life
Streaming throughout me
From the Supreme Being
Dwelling within
Shoring, nurturing the real me
Breaking out, emerging
From my old mold
Blossoming
Breathing, exuding Life unto all
Breathing Being!

OH, MY GOD!

Beautiful
Why would I not be?
Worthy of love
No doubt
Can expect no less
From a facet of God
An expression
Of God's Essence
Which I am
Unique, special
Beautiful
Essential to the puzzle
Of God-Universe
Oh, my God!
God in me
God-me
Unfolding, blossoming
Reaching, connecting
With other God's particles
Of all shapes and forms
'Till God-Universe
Bursts
In the glory of its purpose
Fulfilled!

I AM FROM. . .HAITI

I am from. . . .
Strong black coffee with lots of sugar
And cassava bread to dip in
I am from. . .
Mountains of rice and beans
With fried chicken, beef, or goat
I am from. . . .
Fried plantains and fried pork
With beaucoup pikliz
I am from. . .
Drinking coconut milk
Straight down from the nut
Cool and thirst-quenching
I am from. . . .
Deep blue, warm, tropical ocean
And sandy beaches
I am from. . . .
Sizzling heat
With refreshing sea breezes
And intoxicating cross winds
I am from. . . .
Singing birds and rivers
With me lying down
On dry coconut tree leaves
Enjoying this natural symphony
I am from. . . .
High mountains
Unfortunately losing their green
Over the years
I am from. . . .
A language, colorful and eloquent,
Rich and elegant
Called Haitian Creole
I am from. . . .
Simple life,
With large, close-knit family
With neighbors being part of family
I am from. . . .
Christmas night's reveyon
With music, songs, and prayers
All night long
I am from. . . .
New Year's Day

Eating soup joumou
All day long
With neighbors and family
I am from. . . .
Euphoric carnivals
With people becoming music
On the streets everywhere
For three whole days
I am from. . . .
Vodoo rituals
Drumming , dancing, and chanting
To all gods in nature
I am from. . . .
A mysterious island
With wild zombi tales
Beyond your imagination
I am from. . . .
A fascinating island
Which breeds
Ingenious, resourceful artists of all sorts
I am from. . . .
First black republic
Victorious ancestors
Freedom winners from slavery
Daring, dignified fellow citizens
Still fighting for freedom and justice
I am from. . . .
Life-loving, life-giving
Courageous, proud
Laborious people
With dreams and hope
Working a tired land
Or foreign fields of all sorts
For daily sustenance
And more
I am from. . . .
Hospitable, humorous
Religious, and spiritual folks
Trusting God always
To care for us
Today
And tomorrow
I AM FROM. . .HAITI!!!

A RIVER RUNS THROUGH ME

A river of love
Joy, wisdom, and peace
A river of abundance
A river flowing from Source
River of goods
River of God
Drowning down in its streams
All negative skims
In thoughts, sensations
Feelings, and intentions
A river runs through me
Refreshing, nurturing
Strengthening
Making me whole
Making me one
With everything and everyone
A river runs through me
And the universe
Vibrates with goodness
For all to enjoy

ONCE IN A BLUE SUN

You say blue?
The sun, blue......huh.....
Always pictured
The sun yellow...
'Till today
I noticed
Within its fine
Golden rim.....
The sun is blue!!!
What do you know.....

HURRICANED IN HAITI

Sounds tragic. horrifying

As a child. not for me

Hurricaned in

Enjoying unusual meals

Grilled corn. grilled nuts

Sharing musical tales and riddles

Escapades in the howling wind and rain

Freedom to skip and dance

In nature wild

Oblivious to dangers worried about by adults

Back in only when called

Yet for another enjoyment

Of unusual meals

Grilled corn. grilled nuts

Sharing musical tales and riddles

Some of the simple pleasures

Woven in the tapestry

Of my childhood

Hurricaned in Haiti

HURRICANED IN HOLLYWOOD

Sucked in the big frenzy
From TV
Neighbors, work authorities
Folks in whole city
Experiencing
My first Florida hurricane
Joining all adults
In frantically securing home
Work equipment
Hoarding basic supplies
Riding the suspense of
When it's ought to hit
And when, whether, how it does hit
In the midst of it all
Little me takes over
Running back and forth
In wild nature
To and from neighbor's home
Caught in the middle
Of Katrina, the hurricane's dance
With all around
Then staying put
Hurricaned in
Dreaming of driving
By the ocean next time
To safely contemplate
A hurricane's bold moves
Before, during, and after
Meanwhile, hurricaned in
I am content
To lay back and enjoy the soothing howler
Of the wind and rain
Wrestling with the trees
And power lines

As I eat unusual meals
Dried nuts, canned soup, apples
Suspicious leftovers
At candle light
Sleeping like a log at night
Waking up at 10 o'clock in the morning
Reassuring worried loved ones
I am A-OK
Hurricaned in Hollywood
And yes
The adult me does re-join
The child me
Opening my eyes, ears, and heart
For news of victims
Less fortunate than I
Sending them comforting vibes
Extending and receiving a helping hand
And being grateful that
I am A-OK
Hurricaned in Hollywood

MANGO DELIGHT

Gently cupped
In one hand
Carefully…
As if holding an egg
Slowly I bring it to my face
Closer to my nose
Inhaling the aroma
Stronger and stronger
Then down to my lips
And my teeth
Gently piercing
The mango skin
Peeling it
Soft and smooth
While sweet juice
Bursting and streaming
Between
And all around my lips
Ooh! Aah!
Mango delight
'Till all that is left
Is a big yellow seed
Bitter sweet. . .
And still feeling
The delightful, savory juice
Flowing down inside me
Making its way to my belly
Ooh! Aah!
Mango delight!

I FEEL THE OCEAN BREATHE

Cool, quiet Sunday dusk
At the beach, of course
Comfortably lying
On the warm, moist sand
Caressed from head to toe
By the sea breeze
Taking in slowly
The ocean's
Looks, feels, and sounds
One at a time
Breathing its saline air
And...oh surprise
I feel the ocean breathe
With me
Between its every wave
With the tide
In... and... out
Between my every inhale
And exhale
In... and... out
Together, what honor
As the saline mist
Of every wave
Reaches for my lips
As in a kiss
Prompting my next breath
And the one after....
A breathing dance
Exquisitely intimate
Soul to soul
Little me
With the mighty sea
What a gift!

BREAKFAST WITH A BIRD

At the seemingly sumptuous table
Which is my back yard
In between plush green blades of grass
My winged breakfast date
Is gleaning, savoring
Bits of je ne sais quoi
While I
Leaning on my window
Right next to my winged friend
Slowly and with much delight
My own breakfast
I'm savoring
Delicious blend
Of various tropical fruit juices
And some good-for-you soy milk
Many a time have I watched
M winged breakfast guests
At the seemingly sumptuous table
Which is my back yard
In between plush green blades of grass
Gleaning, savoring
Bits of je ne sais quoi
But today
'Tis my first breakfast date
With a winged friend
In hope of many more. . .

MY PEOPLE. . . ONE TOUCH

My people, Haitian. . .a jewel!
Weaving its talents
With skillful, graceful moves
Into another country
Another language
Yet, keeping its own colors
Its own richness. . .
My people. . . beautiful!

My people. . .spiritual treasure!
Exuding genuineness
Pure, simple joy
The music of life
Exuding hope against hope
My people... so strong!

My people... one touch
Radiating loving energy
Channeling waves of nurturing warmth
With skillful, graceful moves
Into open souls
My people...so profound!

CELL SOUNDS

Sounds, songs from my body cells
I wish...
Sounds of cellular phones all around
I mean...
Zillions of variations
Piercing the air
Wherever, whenever
All fascinating
At times, plain annoying
Bursting in the midst of action or motion
Or even worse
In the silence of being or communing

Sounds of cellular phones
Of the world communicating
Messages of all sorts
Still...
At least we're in touch

FEELING HOT, HOT, HOT

And just loving it!!!
Soft feeling of sweat beads
Bubbling up, racing down
From my forehead, under arms
My face, neck, and thighs
Forming refreshing pearls
Of slightly salty crystal water
Glistening
Steaming and streaming down
Oh so sweetly
Over every which part of my body
Slowly saturating my clothes
Keeping me cool...
Most would say
It's utterly uncomfortable
But I...just ...love...it!!!
One of my life's
Seemingly silly pleasure
Feeling hot, hot, hot!!!

HOLIDAY GIFTS

December twenty-seven

Past the holiday commotion

Which I dislike

Yes, today

In my own way

I am open

To notice and open

Awaiting holiday gifts

In me, to me, to all

 Gifts of various kinds

Forms, feels, and colors

Sounds and smells

Myriad of gifts

In the gift of this moment, space

Of silence

To notice the unnoticeable

The gifts within gifts

God's abundance of gifts

Flowing

In the ocean of my present

Gifts in wrappings of all sorts

Protecting the wonder

The specialness

The pace and timeliness

The purpose

Of the gifts

In wrappings

Transparent or opaque

Colorful or dull

Attractive or repulsive

Harsh or smooth

No matter the appearance

I trust the gift within

Non-returnable, yes

But I trust the Giver
For only what is good
He gives

I move beyond the wrapping
No matter the appearance
To meet and open the gifts
One by one
As they come
In the space of my present
I give thanks and celebrate
My life, my soul
Enriched
It's a gift

LOOK OUT…HE'S DROWNING….

Deep-sea diving
No oxygen
Rarely coming up for air
If only briefly
Got good lungs
He says
And good liver too
Buying time, buying beer
Drunk as a fish
I want out
He says
Yet, still under
Heavy as lead
Pulled down deeper
After every feeble attempt
To escape to dry land
Tomorrow is the day
He says
Everyday
To grab the life lines
And get out
Never happens…
It doesn't stick, the bait
Lifeguards stand by
Helpless
Waved away
Hoping against hope that
Dry land appeal
Will prevail
Someday, somehow
Tomorrow, perhaps
Again he'll come up
And out
For air, for life
Or….
Look out…he's drowning….

COOL CUT

My hair short
Short hair cut
Light, clean, cool
Open for
Caressing, refreshing summer breezes
Gentle skin-throbbing showers
Ocean water
Tickling rain drops
And perhaps
A tender human hand
Sliding through my short hair
Discovering
The feel of softness
Of my hair
Revealing
My face open
With well-defined cheekbones
My face
Beautiful
Content, smiling
In celebration of my hair
Cut real' short
Light, clean
Cool cut!

Y'DID NEFESH

Friend of my soul

My mentor, sacred gift

Here we are

My inner gates opened

And we're set

On this thrilling voyage

On the cusp of my brand new life

As I brave the waves

You hold my hand

Sometimes dancing with me

Twirling me dizzy

Yet, with knowing, caring, gentle hands

Moving with serendipity

Inspired from the treasured depths

Of your seasoned guts

Sometimes like a midwife

Comforting, yet respectful

Attentive to the slightest breath

The faintest whisper

Through the birthing journey

Scuba diving most of the time

So with me

Yet, so ahead of me

To be with me

Just the way I need

Just in time

Enough time

Not missing a beat

Aptly excavating with me

The deepest recesses of my being

Searching with me
Through muck and thorny bushes
Gathering precious omens
Tending to the broken
Gently washing off
Layers of dried blood and mud
Healing the scars
Smoothing rough edges
Guiding my trembling eyes and hands
In discovering, screening, refining
Creating, crafting, connecting
Gradually bringing forth
The unprecedented, ravishing masterpiece
Of the woman in me re-born
Voila!!!

I'VE GOT TO DRIVE!

Comfortably

In my old little Honda

Still. . . for now

Though with no A/C

In hot Florida, mind you

Yet, in style

With my windows down

The wind

Warm or cool

Teasing through

My afro hair

Caressing my skin

On my arms, on my legs

The back of my neck
Oooh! Aaah!

I've got to drive!

I know how

In my old little Honda

Running real good

With basic insurance

Nifty driving record

And protection from Source

The best

Which money can't buy
I've got to drive!

To my anxious spells

I say
Fuck the hell off

I wanna be free

I've got to drive!

DANCING SUNSET

Cloudy sky
Menacing rain
But didn't happen
So I surrender
To my tantalizing desire
Of being in
And communing
With the ocean
My aqua home
And after what seemed
A long, slow drive to the beach
I am in
The right spot
Like in a reserved seat
The best
In my aqua home
Savoring, guess what
A magnificent surprise
A dancing sunset
Yes, the sun, dancing
Amazingly
Dancing its way
Into the night
In between the clouds
Displaying
Its surrounding blend of colors
Breathtakingly sumptuous
Filling me with a sense of the miraculous
So I contemplate
This marvel of nature
Singing and dancing
With the setting sun
Entranced
In this feast of my senses
And of my soul
Another stupendous gift
From my God
Just because. . .

I'M UPSET THAT I'M NOT UPSET

Huh?. . .

I'm upset

That I'm not upset

What?. . .

I'm upset

That I'm not upset

You don't say!. . .

Yep!. . .

Weird and real

I'm upset

That I'm not upset

'Tis the whistle blow

Sounding guilt

Sounding fear

Sounding feelings of unworthiness

From my life's

Ever so intransigent border patrol

My mind!

Cautioning against

My leaps and bounds

Crossing over

From the stinkin' stagnant familiar

To the free-smelling flow

Of Life lived from deep

And lo' and behold

I follow

With my tail of despair

Between the weary legs

Of my soul

Back in my usual stupor

Not yet accustomed

To cruising high altitudes

Yep. . .

I'm upset

That I am not upset
As I spring across however briefly
On the wings of Being
Sniffing a freer me
Blossoming, dancing away
Suddenly... border control!
I'm back again
Upset
That I'm not upset
Weird and real
Waiting once more
To be swept off my mind
To be the one
Blowing the whistle
And my mind
Will follow me home
To sounds of Joy
Sounds of Life
Sounds of Being
Gentle reminders
Of where I truly belong
But. . . meanwhile. . .
I'm upset
That I'm not upset
Huh?. . .
Yep!. . .
I'm upset
That I'm not upset
Imagine that. . .

THE SWAN

Peering at my soul's window
One may wonder
What's going on?
What's the reason
For the commotion?
Major renovation
Going on
Yet, in silence
Only if
Deep down you look
Then you'll see
The sewer
Draining
Into Mother Earth's bosom
All my soul's refuse
For her to process and transmute
Into fertilizer
To nurture life
Metamorphosed
Back to living creatures
In the miraculous cycle
Of birth and death.....and birth...
Then you'll know
Major makeover indeed
For a new swan soul
To flap out her wings
Resonate
With her unique vibrance
Exude
The beauty and richness
Of her unique presence
On human planet
So...
Watch for the opening curtain
And let yourself be
Mesmerized
By this swan of a soul

BEING WITH YOU

Sunday morning...
Relaxing in my bed
New bed, new house, new life
Pondering on my new life
Thinking about. . . no
Being with you
My oasis
In the midst
Of raging, dry, scorching winds
And blinding dust
Of the surrounding contempt
Plowing through my yearnings
For peace and delight
Of my own design

Sunday morning...
Being with you
Breath of fresh air
My breathing space
My steady base
Immersing myself in you
Letting the water of you
Friend of my soul
Refresh every nook and cranny
Of my inner self
God could be jealous. . .
But, no. . .'cause
In you God dwells
God's vessel you are
Infusing love and peace
Healing, nurturing
Human touch
Of superior quality
Marvelous jewel
Of divine incarnation

Sunday morning...
Precious moment
Being with you
Every minute
Savored by me
Slowly, tenderly!

FLYING WITH GOD

Where to?
Nosy me asked
It matters not
Answered God
Just enjoy the ride
And the view
And the feel........
Snuggled in between
God's powerful, great, big wings
I am flying
With God!
What's to fear
Or to resist?
Rather
I fling open my own wings
In harmony
With God's great, big wings
Enjoying the ride
The view, and the feel
Wherever He may lead
Blowing kisses through the wind
To the sun and the moon
The other planets
The stars and the clouds
To birds of all species
People in airplanes
To the ocean down below
To flowers and trees
To all folks on earth......
Flying, I am, indeed!
With ~~~ God
Toward all discoveries
Awaiting me
Where? What?

It's a surprise!
And I'm up
For each and all
'cause
I ~~~ am ~~~ flying ~~~
With ~~~ God

MY AUTUMN GIFT

Didn't suspect a thing
As I traveled to church
On that warm, Floridian Sunday morning
'Till I parked my car
And happened to glance
At the passenger seat
There. . . a perfect autumn leaf
My autumn gift!
Quietly waiting
For me to take notice
All the autumn colors
Blended in that one little leaf
There to surprise me
"Happy Autumn," they say
Even in Florida
A taste of beloved
New England autumn
All the way to Florida
In my little Honda
Just for me!

BABY SOUNDS

A baby.....
In my single's pad?
Oh, yeah......
Not mine
If you must know
At least....not quite
Yet, born in my hands
From my little sister's womb
Her first born
My first time
Witnessing
Such miracle of birth
Peter is his name
And home we come
With adorable, precious little Peter
So perfect!
In the still of the night
His soft, gentle baby sounds
Wake me
And lull me back
Into peaceful sleep
Other times
Feeling his tiny heart
Beat with mine
In harmony
As he lays on my chest
So trusting
Listening to auntie's
Warm, comforting singing
Oh, how sweet it is
The power
Of a baby's
Unconditional love
Peter is his name
My brand new nephew
And he is so-o-o fine!

LOVE PUDDLE

It came down
Long and hard
The rain
Rhythmically quenching
The thirst of Earth
Now the rain has stopped
And the Sun takes over
Slowly sucking
Leftover water
'Round and about
Stubborn puddles
Artistically, in style
That's when I stumble
Over a heart-shaped puddle
The love puddle
I named it
Watching it drying
More and more
Day by day
'Till what's left
Is the earthly bed
Awaiting
The next rainfall
Thirsty Earth, sucking Sun
Stubborn puddle
Of what shape?
We shall see….

WHERE'S MY COUNTRY'S FLAG???

Day labor is over

Night has settled in

About to lay myself to rest

Looking for my Haiti's flag t-shirt

To wrap myself in

As I do every night

As one of my ways

To hold my Haiti around me, close to my heart

As one of my ways to hold my Haiti

In my whole body, my whole being's prayer

For my people's healing

Healing from raging greed

And bitter hatred

From blindness of false power

Sheer oblivion to basic human values

But tonight. . .

My country's flag is missing...

Lost in the flood

Of my people's blood

Lost underneath

Stinkin' piles of trash

Of my country's capital

My country's flag

Melted in the inferno

Of burnt homes, stores,

Schools, tires, and bodies

My country's colors

All muddled

In putrid waste of stagnant sewers

Boarding my country's capital

My country's flag smoked away

With gun shots

Piercing random bodies

Of friends and foes

My country's flag
What became of you?
Any chance of rebirth
For you?
For my people?

My country's flag is missing
And I'm crying. . .
Yes, I'm crying a river
Powerful enough, I wish
To cleanse you back to dignity
To show off your colors once again
Haiti, my Haiti,
For you to emerge
From the abyss of doom
And shine once again
As "the pearl of the Antilles"

DIVE IN THE DIVINE

In the heart of a city
Yet, away
From the usual stagger
Of frantic haste
Of the human rat race
Amidst busy, noisy, rigid
Time, space, things, and folks
There it is…awaiting
An oasis
A cool shul
Where, amazingly
Time, space, things, and folks
Are filled with
True peace, love, and joy
Flowing in cool, refreshing streams
Within, over, and beyond
Time, space, things, and folks
A moment of heaven
A taste of depth
As folks of all kinds
Connect
Soul to soul
In a seemingly
Infinite trance
Of loving, dancing
Singing, drumming
Hugging, laughing
Diving in the Divine
       . . .
Cool shul!

I USED TO BE 48.....NOW I'M 12

Sunday morning
Awake from my night sleep
More importantly
Awake from my forty-eight-year sleep
I spring out into a dance
Celebrating life
Celebrating being 12 years old
Feeling lightness and relief
From the weighed-down
Forty-eight year-old woman
I used to be
Loosening the shackles
Of rules and principles
Shoulds and shouldn'ts
Musts and mustn'ts
Cannots
And don't-you-dare-or-elses
Images to protect and preserve
Responsibilities to fulfill
Oh so important
To be taken so seriously
And serious I've been
So die-hard serious....
In my past forty-eight years
Of laboriously burying the real me
Under bushes thick and tall
Of an ego self
An illusion of me
Molded in my mind
Fed along the way

With thoughts forming a story
From interactions
With those who's, when's
And whereabouts
In those forty-eight years

But today, I'm 12 years old
Feeling joy and wonderment
Finding Easter eggs
In all the death-smelling
Mighty scary-looking
Life situations
Of the forty-eight year-old woman
I used to be
Hauling along those years
Of problems and failures
Anger, pain, and sadness
Guilt, self-pity, and bad luck
Wounds, regrets, and phobias
Should-haves, should-not-haves
Could-haves
What-the-hell-were-you-thinking
Doing, not doing
Wanting, feeling, expecting
What, why, how, how come,
Where, when, if, what if, perhaps
Oh, my God!

But today, I'm 12 years old
Celebrating and playing
Reaching for the roots
Of these coarse, stubborn weeds

Gently holding and twisting
To slowly but surely pull them out
Making space for my real self
To blossom freely
To flow and dance
With everyone
And everything that is
To the rhythm of life-giving music
 From the divine Source
Within me and all

Today, I'm 12 years old
Celebrating
Dancing all over
In my new house
In joy of being
God's spoiled little girl
Opening birthday presents
From gift-bearers
Of all forms, looks, and bearings
People, relationships
Places, events, and things
From now
And from my past
Making each and all
Into new friends
Through this awe-filled
Re-birthing celebration
My life
Is cracking up to be
From those Easter eggs
And I keep making discoveries

In my present
And in my past forty-eight years
As one searches a rubbish dump
For unassuming treasures

Today, I'm 12 years old
Breathing joy, love, and peace
In life's moments
One by one
Freely, naively, openly
Finding delight
In being
God's spoiled little girl

Today, I'm 12 years old
And here you are, too
Friend of my soul
Tuned in with me
Near or far
As I gently
Smell your presence
Or see you in a flash
Sitting right next to me
Being comfort and peace
Quiet and inspiring joy
Affirming, confirming
Spurring me on
With the discreet, perfect nudge
Fitting each moment
Witnessing life dawning
Slowly unfolding

Today, I'm 12 years old
Smiling and laughing
Dancing and playing
With my newly-made friends from my past
Singing for all ears
Reading tons of books
Trusted and trusting
Loving much and being much loved
Learning and growing
In joy of being
God's spoiled little girl

I used to be forty-eight years old
Now, I'm 12
Amazing!

FLORIDA

I heard of a peninsula
Where the sun is hot,
With no real winter
Practically one season
With little variation in temperature
I heard of a peninsula
Where the beaches are
Spectacular and enticing
With an entire nature
Breathtakingly beautiful

I now know of this peninsula
For I've escaped
The northern harsh, cold, long winters
To enjoy my tropical self
In this peninsula
Warm southern climate
All year long
With freedom
Of light body covering
If at all
Sensual breezes
Deep green, luxurious
Magnificent nature surrounding all
With soothing, luscious, invigorating
Communion sessions with the ocean
And more....

I now know of this peninsula
Where I can delight
In being a tropical gal'
To the pith!

MAY I HAVE THIS DANCE?

Now don't be shy
Baby steps are fine
It's a new dance
I know
And you're barely awake

You've danced before
I know
Long and hard
A macabre dance, that was
In the arms of addiction
Sadistic lover
Spinning you dizzy
In the dark clouds of denial
The wind of euphoria
Straight down the pit
Of less and loss
Resonating the terrible thud
Of hitting bottom
And here you are
Alone in your soul
Wounded
Stripped, buck-naked
Or quite close
Ready to clean up and get dressed
I pray
  Wanna recover, don't you?
So then….
May I have this dance?

Now don't be shy
Baby steps are fine
It's a new dance
I know
Take my lead if you will
On this path
Of a new lifestyle
I'll twirl you dizzy
This time with a new high
Of creating a new reality
Dancing new steps
Thundering tango of awareness
Quiet bolero of acceptance

Ballet of humility
Salsa of accountability
Tap dance of forgiveness
Received and given
Konpa of self-care, healthy coping
Rumba of whirlwind change
Waltz of social competence
In the jazz of life
Soon uncovering
New steps of your own

Should you turn your head
And glance
In the mirror of times past
You'll see
Your old lover and dance partner
Lurking its ugly head
Asking you with charming words
Sweet venom
For one more dance
Look back in my eyes
And for you I'll mirror
Truer life

Yet, should you slip
And fall back into its arms
There I'll be to catch you
If you let me
Once, twice, or more times
To resume our dance
Till on your own
To dance away
You're ready
This time
Awake, bold, and responsible
Loving and humble
Rapt with joy and creativity
In the ballroom of your own life

Meanwhile....
Here and now....
May I have this dance?

SPRING & WAR?

It's spring!

Flowers and tree leaves blossoming

End of winter snow and cold weather

Freshness, beauty, colors

LIFE!

Yet, at the dawn of spring

WAR!

Bizarre, isn't it?

Almighty United Sates

Stepping over United Nations

Against Saddam Hussein

Destroying Iraqi people

Explosion of rage and fire

Wreckage, horror, blood everywhere

DEATH!

No time is fit for war

But in springtime?

A more direct, deadly insult

To the value of life

I could think not!

A DAY OFF

A day off
Because of whatever
Or just because
Fresh breeze
Into the hot, hurried routine
A pause in the rat race
Must-do's
Here-and-now-or-else's
This-way-or-you're-fried's
A day off
A breath allowed
To be taken slowly
Space to feel
Me and whatever else
A day off
To be human
To re-connect
With me and whoever else
Quench my thirst
Drink more deeply
Into Source
A day off
To step back
See the real
Past the blur
Of rush, rush, rush
Smell the flowers
Along the very path
Of daily rat race
A day off
To treasure the beauty
Within, around, and beyond
The people, events, interactions
On the very path

Of that daily rat race
A day off
To recharge and be ready
To better serve
With renewed love
And new insights, perhaps
A day off
For a more placid journey
Whether through the race of doing a living
Or
To taste
What it's really like
To be alive
A day off
Ahhhhh!

SWEATY WOMAN

Bright June morning
The sun
Blasting its light all around
I, in my Florida room
Swirling madly
Bumping, grinding
And gliding
To the beat
Of Haitian spirit music
Celebrating the wonder
Of life
Through my morning dance
And I'm sweatin'
Oh…the sensual feel
Of my own water
Freshly produced
Seeping from within
Pearling all over my skin
Forming streams
Getting me drenched wet
Just like after a good round
Of love making as well
Cool, hot, cool

Real women don't sweat?
Ha!
Smelly, repulsive
Not sexy?
I say not human
Don't know what you're missin'
This exhilarating feeling
Of being
Feeling life deeply
Ought to try it sometimes
Wet, real, ecstatic
Sweaty woman!

MOON OVER SEA

So I'm here to see
Yet another treat
After a work week and a nap
Basking in the sea
Softly luminous
From a full harvest moon
Creating silver circles
With the ocean ripples
Intertwined, undulating
Offering a natural spectacle
Of a unique kind
From the supreme romantic
Who promises the moon
And delivers
Elegantly, stunningly
To the knowing eyes
And I am here
With my feet anchored
Deep
Within the sandy heart
Of Mother Earth
Seeing and feeling
The ocean water
On my skin
The moon light
On my moving body
Forming shadows
As I walk by the shore
Kicking the sand
Warm and moist
Over my feet
Or just standing
Taking in everything
The whole gift
Of moon over sea
In full splendor
No other place I wanna be!

ODE TO OLDER SIS

It's Mother's Day
I'm thinking about Mom
Also about all my sisters
Now mothers as well
And you, the first
After Mom
Played mom
To all of us, your sibs
Not that we always
Liked your ways
Nonetheless
With your own children
You show courage
You show faith
Determination to bravado
Ushering them
To every new step
Loving them as well
Through the missteps
From our native country, Haiti
To the U.S.A.
Today is Mothers' Day
And I want to salute
You
My eldest sister

SUNSET ON THE POND

Seven twenty-five!
Still wandering thirsty
In the parched and weary land
Of my life......
My eyes weary of looking
Still searching for.....
The Well of Living Water

Stop! Listen!
A gentle knock on my door I hear
Come on! Let's go out to Nature!
He, at last, lets me hear His voice
And there we go!

We sit down on the ground
God and I
Watching Sunset on the Pond
At seven twenty-five.....

Summertime sunset
The pond is there
Letting the wind open
The layers of its heart
To welcome deep down
The beauties
The magnificent colors of love
In its midst......

How gently the sun penetrates
Mixes its golden rays

With the pond's tender blue
In the most perfect harmony!

Say, golden sun....
What if elsewhere
You were
Giving out your splendor?
No way would your glorious caress
Be welcomed within blue waters!
No symphony of love would be
No delight for my eyes and heart
At seven twenty-five........

But blue waters are right there
Ready to receive
And golden sun is there
To pour in its treasures
And also, this day
Fortunate enough
I too am there
Thankfully watching
Sun and water blending their riches

What a unique jewel of Nature!
Incredible marvel generously offered
By Love
Faithfully
Every day
Whether I am watching or not....
Sunset on the Pond
At seven twenty-five......!

Still seated down on the ground
God and I
Watching Sunset on the Pond
At seven twenty-five.....
His Spirit opens the layers of my heart
To let in the colors of Love
How gently He penetrates
Mixes His own beauties
With mine!
Sharing a more wonderful me
How sweet is His touch! So tender
Forever would I be
Leaning on His heart
"See how much I love you!"
He keeps whispering
Yes, I can see
Through this
Sunset on the Pond
Special gift to me
On this day
At seven twenty-five

Yes, now, only now, looking back
My life I can see
Deeply touched by your presence
Much like the blue waters
Deeply embraced by the golden sun
Yes, there you were
Faithfully
Tenderly

Leading me
Like by a pathway through the sea
And I didn't know it....
And like from a spring
Streams of tears
Were running down my cheeks
May I wash your feet with my tears?
I offered
Let your wish be real
He replies
So I did

By nine
It is time
To check back in
So we do
My hand in His
Treasuring this everlasting memory
Carved in the bottom of my heart
Sunset on the Pond
At seven twenty-five

GREENER & GREENER GRASS

I close my eyes
And I see
I am a lawn
A vast, green, well-cared-for lawn
Being watered
From the roots
By the Supreme gardener
I am a lawn
With a job to just "be"
Keeping every grass blade open
With no fear
Of underfeed or overfeed
Sitting pretty and exuding beauty
 Fragrance of fresh grass
And all manners of fabulousness
I am God's lawn
Where the grass is greener
Day by day
For all to see

BIRTHING LABOR . . . PROLONGED

I wonder with anger
Why a mother
Like my sister
Should have to suffer
For so long
Far from her children
Now older. . .
Could understand a few years worth
Of this unnatural quandary
But definitely not this. . .

How many mother-child events
She's missed. . .
So many birthdays
So many discoveries
Not shared with mother. . .
So many tears not dried
By mother's loving hands. . .
So many bruises not kissed
By mother's healing lips. . .
So much confusion
Unexplored, un-clarified. . .
So many milestones. . .
Multiplied by five
So many questions. . .
Only a mother could answer

So I wonder with anger
Why a mother
Like my sister
Couldn't be granted
To journey with her daughters
As they became women
Imparting onto them
Her wisdom in the matter
Heart to heart,
As she hugs them, each in turn. . .
Why couldn't she be granted
To detect the coy smiles
Of her sons
Falling in love for the first time...

I also wonder with sorrow
How a mother
Like my sister
Will fill the holes
Dug by the irony of life
Whereas my sister
Is finally enjoying the presence
Of her first-born
But, to flee the invisible nest
He is ready!!!

I wonder then with sorrow
Until when
A mother like my sister
Will see an end
To this seemingly
Infinite birthing labor
Until when
A mother like my sister
Will be granted
To give motherly hugs
To all five of her children. . .

But You answer
This mother, my sister
Throughout all these years
Apart from her children
With them, has enjoyed a bond
Infinitely more special
More nurturing on both ends
Than in many a side-by-side
Mother-child relationship
And the ultimate gift, it is
To be thankful for
To be treasured on both ends
To fill the holes
Dug by the irony of life
As she awaits
As we all await
For the mystery of the future
To unfold. . . Your way!
In Your time!

SHABBAT SHALOM

Here in this special place
I come
My oasis
Away and within
My usual
I am here, present
To my Source
To and with friends
Together
Singing and dancing
Immersing in Shabbat
The joy, the peace
The love, the embrace
The blessings of the queen
Shabbat Shalom
Taste of heaven
Light
Flowing deep in my soul
To carry back
Within my usual
Till the next time

L'Cha Dodi
Embrace me softly
I am Shabbat
I am the joy and the peace
The song and the dance
The love and the embrace
The blessings

Shabbat Shalom!

I MISS YOU...

I miss him
Says my heart to my mind
You bet!
Replies my mind
Since our first
Slow, time-stopping dance
Savoring every minute sensation
Of this quietly exhilarating merging
Of our two bodies and souls
In your bachelor pad

Yeah, man
I thought I was just... missing you
Then says my heart to my mind
Get outta of here
And let my 'magination in
Soon I am back in your arms
Re-living this
Slow, time-stopping dance
Savoring every minute sensation
Of this quietly exhilarating merging
Of our two bodies and souls
In your bachelor pad

And as often as I allow it
For a few delectable minutes
Before and during
My morning gratitude dance
I am dancing with you
Savoring every minute sensation
Of this quietly exhilarating merging
Of our two bodies and souls

Yeah, man
I thought I was just... missing you
I am also... with you

I FOUND MY FLAG!

Lost it was
Or so I thought
My Haiti's flag t-shirt
As I make my bed
After a restless night
There it is
Under my pillows
Right under my head
Distraught all the while
Frantically looking for it
Yet, there it is
Lying tall, lying proud
With its colors fluttered
By the anxious winds of my thoughts
Dismayed
Yet, there it was all the while
Subtly rekindling my faded hope
Reminding my bleary heart
'Tis the course of the journey
Of my country, my people
From years in the valley
Of death-smelling chaos
To the refreshing oasis of life
Through mazes of uncanny violence
Prostitution of values
Political schemes
From within and without
All the while
My God!
You were there
Symbol of hope against hope
Rekindling my own
In my country's potential
For positive transformation
Yes, all the while
You were there
Undaunted

SQUIRREL & NUTS

Hello, squirrel!
Got nuts?
Seems like no. . .
Got news for ya. . .
I got nuts, but. . .
Ain't sharin' 'em
With you, eager squirrel
Ain't this nuts?
A human being not sharin'
Beasts me!

BARACK OBAMA

October 23, 2008
An early-voting day
One o'clock in the morning
Lying awake in my bed…
I've got Obama on my mind
Visualizin'
My walk to the polls
In about ten hours
To cast my vote
In this year's US presidential elections
--Since I'll be a poll worker
On general election day
November 4th, 2008--

YES, the first time it is
Since I, a middle-aged woman
Couldn't do this
In my own beloved native Haiti
Not by choice, mind you
But due to long dictatorships
Followed by
My transplant in US soil
While soon after
Things changed
In my native country
When I could actually vote…
And, deep sigh from my guts
I wasn't there…

But now, YES!
For the first exhilarating time
As a citizen of the US and the world
I am voting and my vote counts
For Barack Obama
The very first US black president-to-be
About two-hundred and twenty years
Since the first ever
White President George Washington
But now, Barack Obama
The very first US black president-to-be
Mighty man indeed
Made of the fabric of
Not only black and white racial substance
But I believe of all races
A walking-united-nations-
Filled-with-extraordinary-courage
Kinda man
The second tornadoe force wind

After Martin Luther King, Jr.
To fuel the fire
Under the U.S "melting pot'
And make it true to this name…

Oh…I hear thunder
Thunder of applause, that is
From people in all worlds, affiliations, and eras
Ann Dunham & Barack Hussein Obama, Sr.
Madelyn Dunham
Michelle Obama, Malia Ann, Sasha
Lolo Soetoro, Maya Setoro-NG,
Mohamed Ghandi, Frederic Douglass,
Harriet Tubman, Emmett Till
Elizabeth Cady Stanton, Susan B. Anthony
Lucretia Mott, Steve Biko, Paul Robeson
Malcom X, Rosa Parks, Booker T. Washington
Odetta Holmes, Claudette Colvin
Martin Luther King Jr., Coretta Scott King, Yolanda King
Shirley Chisolm, Jesse Jackson, Nelson Mandela
Maya Angelou, Oprah Winfrey, Al Gore, Colin Powell
The Clintons, the Kennedys, Al Sharpton
Vice-president-to-be Joe Biden
About one hundred and eight members
Of my own extended family and circles of friends
Members of Jewish Temple Adath Or
Your friends and political associates
Your voters, contributors, and volunteers
And so many more
From so many countries
In so many different worlds….
Are thunderously applauding you!

Ok! Ok! Ok!
I get it!
I'm joining in…
With my little big poem

So I get up
Fire up my computer
Savor a few quick sips
Of my no-nonsense ginger tea--
Home-made
With the spiciest ginger I can find--

And at the soothing sound
Of sprinkling rain
In the quiet of the night
Obama on my mind

I heed and embrace the honor
Of being inspired
To write you up
Barack Obama
In this little big poem
With profound gratitude
For you
This immeasurable, invaluable
Human gift
A door flung wide open
Offering to infuse new life
To America and the world

America, are you ready?
World, are you ready?
To receive this man as such
To continue unwrapping the content
Of his heart, mind, and soul
To delight
In the part of God
You are, Barack Obama
And want to keep manifestin'

America, are you ready?
World, are you ready?
To allow this man to meet
And help blossom
The part of God
Each of us is
Finally, slowly, but surely
In his own way
Overcoming the insidious and nasty
Rocks, mud, thorns, and horns
Of our petty resistances
Of all forms and sizes
To positive change
From bottom to top
Instead of the old,
Oppressive style of
From top and
Perhaps, rarely
To bottom

Together, I beg of y'all
Let's heal and keep building
This glorious God-puzzle
America and our world are destined to be
Thank you, Mr. President-to-be
Barack Hussein Obama!

MIDNIGHT RAIN

Still up and alert
Clicking
On my computer
Playing a game of solitaire
My bird clock ticks
Chirps, rather
It's midnight
Giving a signal
And like clock work
Soft and steady
Chimes in the rain
Ushering me to bed
Comfy and relaxed
I am listening 'till
Lulled away to sleep
By the music
Of midnight rain

WITH THIS SMILE. . .I THEE WED

Nervous? Not the least
As it appears, at least
Love all over is written
On these two faces
Smiling eyes and lips
Softly, silently
 Sending waves of love
To each other
Unfettered and unflinching
As if nothing else is needed
To seal this mutual bond
With this smile...
Smile...smile...smile...
I thee wed...
Wed...wed...wed...
Ain't it clear?
Let's celebrate already
These newly wed
Long time merged
Intertwined
For the journey in togetherness
With this smile...
Smile...smile...smile...
I thee wed...
Wed...wed...wed...

FIRE IN MY BELLY

Thought I was there
For the acupuncture needles only
Another attempt to heal
From my driving phobia
Expecting the subtle sting of the needles
Each and every time
Not so subtle at times
This time
A different treat
Tiny cones of moxa
On a bed of salt
Nestled in the small
Of my belly button
Lit with incense sticks
Fire in my belly
Puffing clouds of smoke
So light and fragrant
Like candles on water
Creating ripples of warmth
Spreading in my belly
Slowly
Sensually
Throughout my whole body

Fire in my belly
Suffusing vibrant energy
Pulsating
Throughout my whole body
Fire in my belly
Like fire in my life

TREASURES IN THE MUD

Mud
Like none ever seen
None ever imagined
In worst, sickest of dreams
Mud
Stickier than...
Even gorilla glue
Deep, thick river of
Mud
Ugly, stinky, sticky
Mud
Splashed over me
Splashed over
Each of our soul
Summoning the way
Back to wholeness
Through the
Mud
Yes
Ugly, stinky, sticky
Mud
Holding deep
Hidden pearls of growth
For each
Brave enough to wade in
Ugly, stinky, sticky
Mud
And salvage the goods
Blessing in acceptance
Ugly, stinky, sticky
Mud
Vehicle of some
Perhaps never imagined in wildest dreams
Invaluable, life-enriching
Treasures...... from
Ugly, stinky, sticky
Mud!

THE MANY MOVES OF CECILE

Friday morning...
Standing in the kitchen
Of what is soon-to-be
My last apartment
Leaning on the fridge
Sipping my morning cup
Of no-nonsense ginger tea
Reminiscing on my journey
In this country, the USA
Being schlepped around
In twenty years, so many times
Nineteen to be exact
From one dwelling to another
Uprooted and re-based
Each time attempting
To make a home
With Cecile's tone
To rest my body and soul
Hoping each time
It will be of duration
And all I got
Was a self-awarded Ph.D.
In efficient packing and moving
Leaving behind, each time
A piece of my soul
So, Friday morning...
Gratefully savoring the thought
Rather, the fact that
This is the end
Of Cecile's schlepping about
Attempting to make a home
With Cecile's tone
To rest my body and soul
For it has happened
Finally!
Cecile has a home
With Cecile's tone
To gratefully rest my body and soul
Finally!

FULL MOON PESACH

(Jewish Passover)

There it was on the horizon

Between sea and sky

Ablaze

Giant, magnificent, spectacular

Orange rising moon

Pesach moon

Freedom moon

Rising in its splendor

Ushering me through the sea

From my stifling Egypts

To exhilarating Freedom land

Am I ready?

I'd better be!

Grabbing my timbrels

Songs bursting out of my soul

I leap and jump

Dancing along

The miraculously parted sea

With the Miriams

and Moses in my life

On my way to Freedom

Guided

By the everlasting light

Of the Pesach moon

I AM THE SOIL

Last night
I get fresh cuttings
Of rhododendrons
Place them in various spots of my home
To keep me company
To enliven, purify, beautify
My living space
Friends of my soul, they are
To share much with
From thoughts to music
To laughter and dreams
To my comings and goings
To water as needed
Within my home
Securing little nests of soil
Moist and warm
Through my fingers
For my growing friends

Then comes the morning
Rosh Hashannah
As I meditate
Suddenly
There's this feeling of being the soil
My whole body and self
I am the soil
And right then
Emerges my prayer
Here I am God
The soil…your soil
Plant whatever you please
In me the soil
For this new year
Later with Temple Adath Or
 I celebrate
O serendipity!
There you are again
Disguised as the rabbi
A messenger
Who didn't forget
The message

Stressing your point that
I am the soil

Yes, Lord
I catch your drift
I am the soil
Important omen
To build on
Over and over again
No matter the losses
I am the soil
Womb of new beginnings
Field of creation
Of countless possibilities
Faith in the darkness
I am the soil
So…let's get planting

I'M CRYING A RIVER

I'm crying a river
A river of tears
Gushing out from
The whirlwind pit of my past
Rushing straight to my present
In overwhelming streams
Knocking me down each time
In their passing
Washing out on the shores
Of my present life
Every dry-blooded, stinkin' wound
I've sustained and carried
Along the way
Through my journey thus far
One by one
Through painful pangs
Of my spiritual labor
Intertwined with jubilation
For this exhilarating new life

I'm crying a river
Freeing, healing, nurturing river
Flowing as an enthralling song
Through the rocks and sand
Along the path
Of my journey toward wholeness

RE-BIRTH IN U.S.

Swept out
Of my mother's womb
Taking my first breaths
In this world
On Haiti's soil
I'm Haitian

Growing up
On Haiti's soil
Fed and raised Haitian
Speaking, breathing, walking
Living, smelling Haitian

Swept out
Of Haiti
Taking further breaths
On U.S. soil
Speaking U.S.
Yet breathing, walking
Living, smelling Haitian
Still…

Carried through life in U.S.
Mixing U.S. best
With Haitian best
In me
Still breathing
Sometimes heavy
Sometimes soft
Through bumps and
Of acculturation

'Till one day…
Re-born as a U.S. citizen
I take new breaths
Of new freedoms
Still breathing…

SWEET JUNCTURE

Last night
Like in a castle
Sheltering indoor springs
I enter your soul

Last night
I watch your soul
Open itself
Like a river
Revealing its currents
Moving up and down
Refreshing with much delight
My own soul

Last night
As we talk music
Of me
Of you
I watch the currents
Of your inner river
Flow out through your face
Beaming with crystal pure,
Candid, genuine joy
And integrity

Last night
From this river of yours
I drink
Gradually, deeply, delightfully. . .
And then, oh, joy!
The currents of your river
Reach in my own soul
And with the currents
Of my own river
Merge
Gradually, tenderly, delightfully. . .

A GIFT OF SPACE

Space I love
I desire ...
Space I got
A gift!
Space I need
At this juncture
In my journey
Physical, spiritual space

A gift of space
To be alone
To eat, sleep, and wash
To read and write
To pray and meditate
To rest, relax, and refresh

A gift of space
To listen
Between sound and silence
To the rain, to music
The chirping of birds
The barking of dogs
Vehicles on the roads
Folks moving about
Interacting

A gift of space
To cry and to laugh
To sing and to dance
Madly, freely, wildly
Like a fool

A gift of space
To awaken
To open my soul, my inner space
To search, to excavate
To unfold

To allow, to welcome
To discover, to marvel
To observe, to wonder
To listen
To mull over, to ponder
To discern
To learn and to know
To experience
To own and to hone
To cherish
The gift of me

A gift of space
To be present
To feel
To re-learn to be
The real me

A gift of space
For God's
Spoiled little girl
To connect with Being
To heal and forgive
To be nurtured and challenged
To grow and to blossom
As the real me
To choose, to respond
To be nurturing
In my space
And others' space

A gift of space
To come home
To enjoy, to treasure
A space to live!

MESSAGE FROM THE GASH

Alas.........

Braving the twinges in my heart

The spasms wringing my guts

The anger poisoning my soul

Still puking

Agonizingly making my way

Down below

All the way to the wound

Inflicted upon me

By you, one of my own

And now....

There at the gash

Dauntlessly

Still puking

I place my ear

Against the still-bleeding open wound

No longer asking why

Listening rather

For...a message there must be

For my highest good

And yours

And it spoke to me

The gash

As it never did before

Or perhaps

As I never listen before

Sapient words

A tale of growth

Recounting stories of choices

Necessary sequences

In the course of journey

In humanity

Yours and mine

Immense lesson

For me to learn
Gazillionth opportunity
 For you
To awaken and manifest
The God in you
So.....
Braving the twinges in my heart
The spasms wringing my guts
The anger poisoning my soul
Still puking.....
I lay myself
In the gash
Immersing in its pool
Of blood and pus
Blending in my tears
Of hurt and rage
Gently stroking its walls
Allowing it
To make me whole again
Sending healing vibes
To you
So you too may emerge
From your own pit
Radiantly manifesting
The God in you

LOVE. . . WHERE?

Some think love is. . .
Nowhere to be found
Or only in certain specific
Proper places. . .
Stop and think more
And you'll find that
Like wind
Like spirit, like fire
Like electricity, like water
Like heat, like cold
Like God
Connecting two beings
Be it in nakedness of material poverty
Or surrounded by luxurious comfort
In the nothingness of a desert
Or in the midst of a crowd
Surviving a storm of any sort
Or immersing in peacefulness
Jumping for joy
Or crying one's eyes out
In freedom or in captivity
In light or dark
High or low places
Young or old
Love can be found to live
Everywhere, anywhere
So said a friend
And I thought it wise
And profound
Just like love itself. . .
Can't touch it
But, sure as life
It will touch you
Long and deep

CAT OF LIMITLESS LIVES

But who's counting?
The gazillion times
I've run
And jumped up
As high as my longing
As fiercely as my desire
To get *me* back
To live fully...
And fell flat
On my buns
Or on my face
Rarely on my feet
Sadly
Lay there for while
Down and out
Bruised and weary
Yet undaunted
Gotta get *me* back. . .
 And bracing again
For another leap
Of faith or dare
Same thing
And another one. . .
Another one. . .
One more. . .
But who's counting
For
Cat of limitless lives
I am
Faith or dare
I'll risk one other life
And another one...
Another one. . .
One more. . .
'Till I get *me* back

Land on buns, face, or feet
Bruised and weary
But not for long
Before the next leap
Leaner, yet stronger
I become
And so it goes
Again and again
But, who's counting?
Cat of limitless lives
I still am

A ROSE FOR OBAMA

'Tis Inauguration Day
Of the 44th U.S. President
Who is none other than
Barack Hussein Obama
The 1st ever Black President
Of the United States of America
And I am
Dressed for the supreme occasion
In my oversized
Obama & King shirt
Elated, restless
I wake up early
Venturing out
In my back yard
To embrace Mother Nature
Before waltzing
Through my special-for-the-day
Morning gratitude dance
I glance over my rose bush
Et voila!
A single rose greets me
"A rose for Obama"
I quickly exclaim
Soon, this rose
Is cut
Placed in a vase
In front of an Obama picture
Smiling large
Like the man himself
Adding to my personal
Celebration
Of a man, a Black man
A people
An unprecedented
Monumental historical event
My humble tribute
Among others
To the new U.S. President
The 44th and…
The 1st Black President ever
Of the U.S.A.
This rose is for you
Mr. President!

FLOATING LIGHTHOUSE

What do you want?
You ask me
With gentle, challenging voice
Like a sourcier
Digging fiercely, caringly
Determined to find water
The essence of my soul
My unique gift or gifts
Deep down below
The surface of my despair
Confusion and pain
What do you want?
You insist
Then came the answer
Bursting out from my guts
With joyous energy...
I want to touch the soul
Of the world
With the poems from my soul
To help make this earthly adventure
A dance with steps
Inspired from within
Our ocean of diverse gifts
I want to touch the soul
Of every being
Like a floating lighthouse
Shooting out beams of light
All around
From the Divine light
So that no one will be out of step
Rather waltzing smoothly
Beaming richly toward
Becoming, once again,
One Light
With various tones

SHELLFULLY YOURS!

Once upon a delectable moment in time
Spring break for niece
Brief escape from work worries for auntie
For a precious, delightful walk together
On beloved Hollywood beach, Florida
There they were, auntie and niece
Teaming up in gleaning beautiful shells
Ooh.....Aah.....Wow......
This one is so special
That one, oh my.....so very pretty
This other one, ant that other one, and that other one
What lovely, delicate shapes and nuances......
And suddenly
Niece finds herself so very......shellful
Thus beaming with shellful joy
And.....you guessed it
As auntie and niece stoop
To collect shells at every step
Niece becomes shellfuller........shellfuller......and shellfuller
Then, much too soon, alas
Time has come to rejoin Mom and Dad
Auntie and niece walk back to the car
Saying a regretful goodbye
To the rest of the shellful world by the sea
Musing with nostalgia already
Why do special moments fly by so fast?
Luckily, in both of our hearts
Shellful joy is forever treasured
To be savored once in a while
Defying time and space

ETERNAL SOUL

I wish to fly inward
Take a dive
Through and through
My soul's earthly journey
Visiting each and every Cecile
Find the links
Oh so mysteriously beautiful
Fascinating
Be able to recognize
And embrace me
In each and all
The African queen with a long red dress
The short-lived prince
The English race car driver
The children's Haitian book store owner
Often sitting on the floor
Gleefully reading to a circle of children
The dutiful grown son
Riding his motorcycle
Through breath-taking foliage country
Who died on his way to visit his mother
The rich woman in love
With her horse carriage driver husband
Living happily together to the end

Yeah…
I wish I could take this dive
In my past lives
See the finished and the unfinished
And learn the tasks of this life
Pull it all together
Past, present, and future
Take it all to my now
Feel and treasuring the wholeness
Carrying it always
In my every now
From this day forward

THE SUN & ME

To the rendez-vous
Us both faithful
I, in my comfy recliner
The sun, right above
Embracing my all
With rays
Golden, warm, and bright
Like a shiny, light, flowing silk robe
Powerfully comforting presence
Every morning or evening
We meet
The sun and me
So far apart
I mean light years far
Yet, joining our energies
The sun and me
So far apart
Yet so close

BABY STEPS

My house he chose
As the lucky ground
For this milestone
The awaited excitement
Of a baby's first steps
His very first ones
In my house
I'm so honored
First steps
Moving around
As a complete human being
Baby Jens is walking!
Welcome to the journey of life
May your every step taken
Into the dance of growth
Keeps you smiling and laughing
With the same innocence and genuineness
You graced my house and life
Forever treasured
On its floor, within its walls, and in my heart
Baby Jens, thank you!

BEAUTY IN TRAGEDY

Dare I say?
Dare I even think?
In the midst of tears
Shattered homes and lives
Drowned bodies
Broken hearts, fear, and despair
Dare I talk about
Beauty in nature's fury
Yet, it exists
And thank God, it does
In fire wherever
Gigantic ocean waves in hurricane
Energetic rush of flood water
Hot, colorful river of volcano ashes
Macabre dance of earthquakes
Bellowing, knock-out winds of tornadoes
To name a few...
Beauty in tragedy
I dare say
Thank God, it exists
Profound mystery
Of a deeper meaning
To reality
The cycle of life
And beauty, like its Source
Shows anywhere
As awakening blows
From life's eclectic variety
Of molding tools
God's natural bulldozers
So, human bulldozers
Please cease
A higher calling we have
In the womb of chaos,
Of nothingness left open
By Nature 's bulldozers
The Word is spoken
Be my guests
Says God
To you and me
Incessantly birthing us
With us, if we will
The beauty we are

The beauty that is
From the very chaos
Brought forth by nature's bulldozers
If we move when nudged
To be God's co-creators
Of our new world
Of our new selves
As the Word is spoken
To birth new life
Beauty
From tragedy

(In homage to all affected directly and indirectly--survivors and deceased-- by recent tsunami, hurricanes, tornadoes, earthquakes, US-Iraq war)

GIOVY, THE MAN

Only 13. . .yet

Mature and resilient

Resourceful

Placidly moving

With the particular ebb and flow

Of various events

Harsh or pleasant

Of your particular family life

Only 13. . .yet

Smooth operator

Magically

Making lemonade

Out of the lemons

Thrown in your young life

Feeling special

No matter what

And indeed, you are

Giovy, the man

So very special

TWENTY-FIVE YEARS IN THE U.S.A.

Something was brewing
In my heart
I knew it
A celebration of a life span
Twenty-five years
In this so-called melting pot
Of a country
Which, still too often
 Looks like
A reluctant juxtaposition
Of people who don't really want
To be together
Truth be told, though
Heroic steps have been taken
To birth change
And it shows
Otherwise you wouldn't be reading
This poem from me
A black-skinned person from Haiti
So, yes this so-called
Melting pot of cultures
Keeps on heatin'
And the various cultures
Are indeed slowly but surely meltin'
For there are still some who want
To be meltin'
While preserving identities
And I am proud to be one
Willing to do just that
Twenty-five years today
Since I be dancing
In this American pot………

94

MY BIRTHDAY ROSE

A lone rose on the bush
It was
Progressively blooming
Day by day
'Till my birthday
How miraculous
And what miraculous timing

And from my window
Every day I watch
The growth
The unfolding
Of every petal
Yet, can't only look from
The inside of my home
Gotta go out to visit
And slowly inhale
The sweet fragrance
Of my birthday rose

Am I cheating?
I wonder
Enjoying my blossoming
Birthday rose
Days ahead
Of my special day
What-ever…I say

And The Day comes
Finally
I rush out first thing
Pick it
Thank the bush
And the Supreme Romantic
Who graciously
Birthed and nurtured this rose

To blossom
Right on time for my birthday

I bring my birthday rose inside
In a vase
Filled with rain water
Nurturance
From its own home
I welcome this precious gift
As it honors and perfumes
Me and my home
On my birthday and
As long as it may

I gaze at my birthday rose often
Take frequent whiffs
Converse with it
Inhaling its fragrance
And the message
Of openness and growth
Timing, patience, and wisdom
Faith and enlightened risk
In allowing
My own beauty
To blossom
Petal by petal
Gift by gift
In gratitude and joy
'Till I become...
My birthday rose
For all to enjoy

IT HAD TO BE YOU!!!

Slowly awaking
From that kind of
Cecile's deep sleep
At the sound of your voice
Floating its way
All the way
Into my consciousness
Into my heart
Like a river
Gently waking every part of me
One by one
Delighting me
In every fiber of my being
Slowly, tenderly
As only you know how
So well, so tenderly
Right away I knew
It had to be you!!!
If only. . . YOU knew. . .

LE TOMBEAU VIDE

(The empty tomb)

Empty, so empty
My life, my soul
Could it be more so
Could I stand it more so
This scary hole
Could I stand the wait
To satiate my hunger
For substance
For life
To fill that scary hole
To feel whole
Dare I wish for such
Or do I wait
To be engulfed
In dead silence
In this hole
One thing I can say
His tomb was empty
'Cause from death he rose
Guess, against fear
I'd better hope
Then I too will rise up
Whole
Rather than sink in the hole
Of my empty tomb

YAEL IN YARIS

One gentle touch
On the remote gismo
And the doors unlock
Inviting me
To take the driver seat
In my brand new
Toyota Yaris '09
I hop in and
Sit in comfortably
Crank up the engine
It softly roars
And I shift
Seatbelt on
To drive
Cruising about town
Happy go-lucky
Enjoying
The feel of new
Safe, comfortable
Absolutely red
My beautiful new car
Yael in Yaris
For another twenty years
Like my good old Honda
Who knows?
Meanwhile
I am starting anew
Yael in Yaris

HOMAGE TO AN UNKNOWN DEPARTED

Something's missing. . .
This morning, yea-a-ah
Something's definitely missing. . .
What? I do not know
You? I did not know
Yet, to your funeral I went
To pay my respects
To a great, kind, sweet, smart, happy,
Compassionate, friendly woman of Haiti
So I've heard over and over
On the radio waves
Where you've made
Some of your marks most profound
Many lives you've touched in a special way
So I've heard over and over

But, this morning. . . I saw and believed!
A myriad of cars
A sanctuary overflowing with sad faces
A voice from afar
Struggling to express
That which is impossible to express
So this morning. . . I saw and I believed!

Something's missing, though. . .
What? I do not know
Outside, I watched the sky crying
On a Sun-day, mind you. . .
In the Sun-shine state

Something's missing. . .
Inside I keep busy
Put on comfortable clothes
Change the music
Make my delicious morning shake

But darn!
Something's still missing. . .
What? I do not know
You? I did not know
Yet, I am touched. . .

SOMEONE's missing. . .YOU!

STUBBORN STUMP

A tree I once was
Yes, before Wilma, the hurricane
Whole, tall, and proud, I was
Now nothing but a stump
A stump, nevertheless
Resilient
Standing bold
Just as before
Tender leaves
Budding and blooming
From every nook and cranny
On my shrunk trunk
A tree I once was... and still am
Becoming once more
For life never dies
Even in a stump
As I only appear to be
Yet, holding in my bosom
A real tree, whole, tall, and proud
Once more becoming…

CHRISTIE IN THE RAIN

Just like her grown auntie
Sweet girl rain lover
Bathing suit on
Dressed for the occasion
To play in the rain
The very games she would play
Indoors dry
Christie in the rain
Drops of rain forming pearls
Cascading down
Her long, dark hair, eyebrows, and smiling lips
Christie in the rain
Free, happy, light
In her element
A joy to be
A joy to watch
Just like her grown auntie

LOVE GRASP

Waking from your slumber
At the sound of my voice
Traveling the airwaves
To reach your ears
To reach your heart
You sound so mellow, so dreamy
We talk small talk
While sliding through
Bits of tender feelings
From time to time
Timidly but surely
And as we waltz
Through this dance
Time also flutters away
Boldly and surely
Yet enmeshed we are still
Into each other's utterances
Both reluctant to say the "g" word
The moment comes, though
Where our heavy, sandy eyes
Takes over and forces us
Into the silence of the night
Yet, for while, as I fall asleep
My hand held onto the phone
As if holding you hostage
In a most enthralling
Enduring embrace. . .

HOME WITH THE OCEAN

My home
The castle of my dreams
Now my home for real
Nestled as a crescent
Multi-dimensional crescent
In a panorama with the ocean
From every window
Of every room
With the ocean I can be
Gazing, communing
Being one with
The ocean, God, or another
In or out of my castle
There I am
With the ocean
Immersed
Physically or from afar
Soulfully embracing
The ocean
I am home
With or in
The ocean

TO BE A WOMAN

To be a woman
To be me
The woman I feel
The woman I'm knowing
What's it like
You ask

So I ponder...
On the many colors
I wear
Interwoven

To be a woman
To be me
The woman I feel
The woman I am knowing
Black and Haitian
Single and childfree
Immigrant and living alone
Educated and fun-loving
Independent-minded
Sometimes assertive
Other times scared
Very scared...
Vulnerable

To be a woman
Performing my life act
In various worlds

With men
Considered first class humans
Everywhere
Except at various degrees
Of glare

To be a woman
A Haitian woman
To be asked
By family and society
Whatcha doing
Being single
What if you get sick
Who will take care of you?
You need a man
For you're a woman
And a woman
Can't be alone
No kids? Well…
A real woman, you're not

And the men and society
Muse
Something must be wrong with ya
A childfree woman?
Must be selfish
Or pitifully barren
Must be a slut
Or a frigid one
Independent-minded?
Danger!

Won't take care of her man
Or keep a man
Meaning
Won't serve him as a maid
And blindly obey him
Will want to wear the pants
Potential overthrow
Stay clear!
Or. . .be with her
If you lust
Or if you must
Provided you're allowed
But. . .on your lion-tamer-toes
At all times you must be

To be a Haitian woman
Courting a man?
Enthusiastic lover?
Must be a slut
Or a desperate crone
For you're not allowed
You're a woman!

What's it like
You ask
To be a woman
Immigrant and black
Educated and Haitian
In the U.S.
Some locals stumble
On the black-immigrant-Haitian-woman face

To be treated
Not only less than men
But plainly less than...
Still, a few look further
Catch a glance
And value
The substance and beauty
In the woman I'm knowing
They're family, in-laws
Friends, colleagues
Or empathetic and savvy
Fellow Haitians

Still probing further. . .
Feels like what?
You may ask
To be a woman
The woman I am
The woman I'm knowing
Performing my life act
Waltzing through
Various reactions and interactions
To the woman I present
In my various worlds

I ponder and. . .
I'll say
I hate menstruation
God owes me an explanation
Thank God for menopause
I'll say

It's a gruesome feeling
Being treated
As second class human being
In all the nasty colors
Only with varying
Density and glare
Yet, taking comfort
In believing
It can get better
Provided I keep knowing
And I hold the knowing
Of the woman I am
With the few in numbers
Growing slowly but surely
Keeping the hope that
More women and men alike
Will learn and hold the knowing
Of the true value
Of being a woman
Sensitive and compassionate
Enjoying the space
Psychological and physical
Of being single and childfree
As a gift from God
Immersing joyfully in nature.
My larger home
So I may keep knowing
The woman I am
The woman I am meant to be
Though at times feeling lonely
Yearning for genuine intimacy

For true, companionate love
Whether it happens or not
Longing to further know my mission
To embrace it and live it
Through my every breath
With the love and passion
Of being me
A giving, fun-loving woman
A woman-warrior
With little tolerance
For untruth and injustice
Hard-working and exuberant
Passionate and trustworthy
Courageous and perseverant
Undaunted
Dancing away my fears
'Till I allow myself
To be
The woman I am
The woman I am meant to be
To myself
And to the world
Imparting
With other willing women
The necessary woman gift
Life-giving and nurturing
At every opportunity
While the separating curtains
Between men and women
Are being pushed away
Further and further

To allow harmony
Between the masculine and feminine
Colors of human richness
To blossom
Fuller and fuller
For a more vibrant-living
Fulfilled world

To be a woman
The woman I am
The woman I feel
The woman I'm knowing
What's it like
You ask

Well, I'll say
I'm still knowing...

MORNING GRATITUDE DANCE

My CD player cued
To the first song of an album
By Alabanza
A Haitian choir
Singing in troubadour
My feet
Adorned with my solar-system-painted socks
Symbolic of
My carrying our whole planet
Through my gratitude dance
For LIFE
In all forms
And from all sources
I glide here and there
Jump, pause a few times
My eyes open or closed
I'm there, moving about
In my Florida room
Doing my morning dance
I am music
I am gratitude
I am joy

I glance through one of my many windows
And see my diverse trees dancing too…
And who's buzzing on my jasmine tree
A gorgeous blue and gray
Dance partner butterfly
He danced around my jasmine tree for a while
Throwing me a few flirting winks
Then left…..
And later
I'm still dancing
And my butterfly friend
Came back

With a few more winged friends…
The more the merrier
I say
And the dance goes on
With my friends
Of all kinds
Butterfly and company
Even with, in spirit
My long-gone ancestors
In the peaks and valleys
Of Haitian mountains
At the sound of drums and conch shells
Brewing a revolution
Birthing new life
Freedom for a country of slaves
I am dancing with all
Celebrating life
In all forms and from all sources
For me and everyone
Gliding away
To the sound
Of Alabanza